# Prompts

Tawnya
Selene
Renelle

What began as a way to remember the things I wanted to write about became something more after the first day of transcribing my handwritten words to type.

It became a catalogue of time spent in lockdown.

It became a catalogue of my experiences.

And then it became a series of prompts? Invitations to you, the reader.

And then it became an essay? An essay about life.

And then it became a collection of poems?

Number One: After another walk in the park that can't be numbered because there are so many and after reading *Ongoingness: The End of a Diary* by Sarah Manguso.

Write about what it will be like to not be a mother.

Write an essay called 'The Cock Healer.'

Use 'Wily.'

Wily.

Write about the ache of your stomach in the morning.

Write about K.

Don't write about K.

Write a response.

Respond.

Use 'Responsive.'

Write about the way the rubbish bin smells.

Write about the man who cares for the swans.

Use a blue pen.

Write about the upstairs neighbours having sex.
  About the intimacy you miss.
  About feeling like your ears steal their privacy.
  About how you sometimes turn up the telly.
  About how sometimes you mute it.

Write about not writing.

Explain the smell of sweat.

Explain the desire to be noticed.

Use 'Paradox.'

Paradox.

Write about the turned over paper crane.

Write about stacks of books.

Write about Hunger.
       About *Hunger* the book by Roxane Gay.
       About hunger for food.
       About hunger for touch.

Use 'Hunger.'

Hunger.

Explain how clean socks feel.

Write about orgasms.

Ignore sentences.

## Number Two: After sleeping in while drinking a second cup of coffee.

Write about nuclear proliferation.
    About hazmat suits.
    About Chernobyl.

Write about trimming pubic hair.

Write about another rainy day.

Use 'Know More.'

Know more.

Know.

More.

Write about glass figurines on the window ledge.

Write about the sound of the rubbish trucks.

Write about advertisements on your phone.
    About the weight loss pills.
    About the makeover game to make a girl beautiful.
    About the cat treats.

Explain the pain in your big toe.

Explain the pain in your shoulder.

Use a yellow highlighter.

Write about Y and W.

Don't write about J, N, or P.

Write about mess.


Write about standing in front of the mirror.
    About lifting your shirt and poking your stomach.
    About staring too long.

Use a stapler.

Explain loss.

Write about cold hands.

Write about circulation.

Use 'Aureole.'
    *Aureole* the book by Carole Maso.
    Aureole the word.
    Aureole, yours.

Explain list making.

Explain scraps of paper.

Write about wanting.
    About wanting less.
    About wanting more.
    About wanting something.

Write about armpit hair.

Write about postcards.

Write about watering plants.
    About watering.
    About water.

## Number Three: After a trip to the pharmacy and charity shops.

Write about your right hip.

Write about window displays.

Use 'Desire.'

Desire.

Write about accents.

Write about sound.
    About buses.
    About clanking bottles.
    About wheels in puddles.

Explain excess.

Write about latex-free condoms.

Write about When *The Sick Rule The World* by Dodie Bellamy.

Use 'Disappear.'

Disappear.

Write about witches.

Write about coffee.
    About two cups of coffee.
    About a percolator.

Write about knitting.

Write about routine.

Use 'Decay.'

Decay.

Explain how it gets in there.

Explain how it doesn't.

Don't explain.

Write about awkward journals.

Write about vests vs tank tops.

Describe isolation.

## Number Four: After doing the dishes, taking out the rubbish, and sweeping the flat.

Write about words.

Don't write about words.

Write about wet pillows.

Use 'Control.'

Control.

Write about talking.

Describe anticipation.

Write about clean clothes.
  About hanging them on the radiator.
  About the way they smell.

Explain patience.

Write about your knickers.

Write about scales.

Write about embarrassing choices.

Write about itching.

Use a red pen.

Use 'Unexpected.'

Expect.

Don't Expect.

Write about absence.

Write about the snowflakes on your window.


Write about hair.
        About your hair being too long.
        About your hair being too short.
        About your hair on the floor.

Write about Audre Lorde.

Always write about Audre Lorde.

Explain tenderness.

Write about fake plants.

Describe the turning of the page.

Write about the body in pain.
        About the book by Elaine Scarry.
        About your body.

Write about hiccups.

Write about sensory overload.

Use 'How To.'

How to.

# Number Five: While traveling on a train for the first time in two months.

Describe squeaking.

Write about being without signal.

Write about your tights.

Use 'Movement.'

Move.

Write about tolerance.
    About how it sometimes feels patronizing.
    About how it insufficiently describes how you feel.

Write about trees.

Explain the colour green.

Write about M.

Write about *Unicorn* by Amrou Al-Kadhi

Write about your reflection.

Write about home.
    About multiple homes.
    About no home.
    About home as desire.
    About home as necessity.

Describe clouds.

Write about privilege.

Use 'Getting There.'

Get there.

Explain flight.

Write about spots of sun.

Write about Turner.
        About Turner, the painter.
        About Turner, Tina.
        About Turner, Florence.

Use 'Turn.'

Turn.

Write about moss/lichen on rocks.

Write about D.

Explain enclosure.

Explain in closure.

Explain closure.

Use 'Closer.'

Close.

Write about nostalgia.

## Number Six: After being held for the first time in two months.

Write about bonds.

Write about skin.

Explain casual.

Write about family.

Use 'Together.'

Don't use 'Together.'

Write about conversations.

Write about warmth.

Describe comfort.

Describe a heartbeat.

Write about understanding.

Write about kinship.
    About kinship you make.
    About kinship you build.
    About kinship you miss.

Use 'Satisfied.'

Satisfy.

Describe forgiveness.

Write about silence.

# Number Seven: After a hot shower and a moment alone.

Describe inappropriate texts.

Write about patterns.

Write about abundance.

Use a piece of tape.

Write about laughter.

Use 'Laughter.'

Laugh.

Explain regrets.

Write about lights.
> About lights that glow.
> About the light of a face.
> About the lightness of your mind.

Describe a single candle on the table.

Write about the weather.

Use 'Show and Tell.'

Show.

Tell.

Explain pointed.

Write about interrogations.

Write about your tattoos.

Write about your ring finger.
        About your middle finger.
        About your pinky.

Use 'Sense.'

Sense.

Use red ribbon.

Write about a shed.

Write about reminders.

Don't write about travel.

Describe before.

Describe after.

Write about how.

# Number Eight: After meeting a writer, one who has reached massive commercial success.

Describe fear.

Write about the future.

Don't write about the past.

Use 'Liberally.'

Liberate.

Write about plenty.

Write about ambition.

Explain community.

Write about standing in line.
      About the food bank.
      About power being shut off.
      About free meals and clothes.

Write about pyjamas.

Write about building.

Describe planning.

Use 'Planning.'

Plan.

Use your own voice.

Your own voice.                 Explain imposter syndrome.

# Number Nine: After Scotland's announcement of another lockdown and finishing Unicorn by Amrou Al-Kadhi

Write about hereditary.

Explain tradition.

Write about guilt.

Write about fortune.

Describe contagious.

Write about wishful thinking.

Write about secrets.

Use a 2021 calendar.

Don't use a 2021 calendar.

Explain futile.

Write about fatigue.

Write about an owl looking for a mate.

Use 'Queer.'

Queer.

Write about drag.
    About drag, the art form.
    About drag, the word.
    About drag.

Write about investigation.        Describe the different ways you cry.

# Number Ten: After being in a crowded place after months of going nowhere.

Write about forgetting.

Write about precaution.

Explain anxiety.

Write about the moon.

Write about noise.

Use 'Strange.'

Strange.

Write about kindness.
> About kindness to strangers.
> About kindness among family.
> About kindness to yourself.
> About quiet kindness.

Describe expectations.

Don't describe expectations.

Write about looking.

Write about the Saturn-Jupiter conjunction.

Explain your star sign.

Write about your uterus.

Use 'Pacify.'

Pacify.

Write about tea.

Write about the snap when pill boxes close.

Write about

# Number Eleven: On an emotional anniversary of a death.

Describe mourning.

Explain mourning.

Write about mourning.

Don't write about mourning.

Write about support.

Use 'Need to Know Basis.'

Need to know.

Know.

Write about plants on graves.

Write about a desire to be cremated.

Write about ashes.

Use 'Loss.'

Loss.

Write about relief.

Write about Nat King Cole.
    About the voice of your childhood.
    About how you remember.
    About what you miss.

Write about cookies.

Describe missing.

Write about hugging your grandmother.
    About how you haven't in over a year.
    About how you can't imagine how it will feel when you do.

# Number Twelve: On New Year's Day 2021

Write about nothing.
    About nothing changing.
    About nothing as a way of being.
    About nothing as a state of mind.

Write resolutions.

Don't write resolutions.

Use the past.

Use the future.

Write about the present.

Write about dancing.

Describe a shift.

Write about what is the same.

Write about letters.

Use 'Patience.'

Patience.

Write about mashed potatoes.

Write about bedding.

Describe sleep.

Use 'Reward.'

Reward.

Write about last year.

Don't write about last year.

Make a list.
        A list of this.
        A list of that.
        A list of whens.
        A list of becauses.

## Number Thirteen: After nearly falling on the icy pavement.

Use 'Be Careful.'

Be careful.

Careful.

Write about cold.

Write about warmth.

Write about ice.
>About ice on the inside of your windows.
>About ice on the streets.
>About ice that is broken.

Describe fog.

Write about skating.

Use 'Kerfuffle.'

Use 'Tenuous.'

Use 'Whoopsie-Daisy.'

Whoopsie.

Daisy.

Write about boots.

Don't write about boots.

Write about putting away.

Write about storage.

Describe process/processing/processed.

Write about whisky barrels.

Write about Gertrude Stein.

Write about never.

Don't write about forever.

## Number Fourteen: After finishing reading *Sphinx* by Anne Garrèta.

Write about memory.

Write about Paris.
  About Montmartre.
  About Musee d'Orsay.
  About baguettes for breakfast.

Describe time disappearing.

Write about needing someone.

Don't write about needing someone.

Use 'Heartfelt.'

Heartfelt.

Write about A***.

Describe coral.

Write about nowhere.

Write about somewhere.

Write about the plant growing out of a building.

Write about not writing.

Use 'The Body.'

The body.

Write about absence, again.

Write about dough.
       About the smell of yeast.
       About the rising.
       About kneading.

Use 'Rise.'

## Number Fifteen: After white supremacists stormed the capitol.

Write about anger.

Write about shame.

Write about helplessness.

Use 'Livid.'

Livid.

Write about double standards.

Explain.

Use 'For Fuck's Sake!'

For Fuck's Sake!

# Number Sixteen: After a walk in the snowy park and buying yogurt to make pear poppyseed loaf.

Write about Winter.

Write about holding hands.

Write about oatmeal.

Use 'When.'

When.

Don't use 'If.'

Write about Alexandra Park.

Describe quiet.

Write about miscommunication.

Write about your nose.

Write about a private smile.

Use 'Nod.'

Nod.

Describe excitement.

Write about noise.
    About the noise of yelling downstairs neighbors.
    About the telly of upstairs neighbors.
    About the noise of frustration.

Explain in the middle.

Write about enjoyment.

Write about crunching.

Write about Index *Cards* by Moyra Davey.

Use 'Proximity.'

Proximity.

Approximate.

Write about baking.

Write about extra.

Describe luck.

Write about classical music.

Use 'Interruptions.'

Interrupt.

## Number Seventeen: After a slow morning of watching RuPaul's Drag Race and reading *Body Geographic* by Barrie Jean Borich.

Write about maps.

Write about mapping.

Write about geography.
	About the geography of yourself.
	About the geography of absence.
	About the geography of geography.

Use 'Sensuality.'

Sensual.

Write about Edith Piaf in the snow.

Write about Edith Piaf in the kitchen.

Describe melting.

Use 'Longing.'

Long.

Write about feeling your face turn red.

Write about children's laughter.

Write about what it is.

Explain fabulous.

Use 'Bravery.'

Brave.

Use a collection of sticks.

Write about bonds.


Write about being fierce.
      About being fierce for others.
      About being fierce for yourself.

Describe lingering.

Use 'Lingering.'

Linger.

# Number Eighteen: After taking a walk in the Winter sun to buy vegetables and while listening to your first ever podcast.

Write about waiting.

Write about not waiting.

Use 'Become Accustomed.'

Become Accustomed.

Write about being fat.
    About being fat buying carrots.
    About being fat buying cake.
    About being fat walking up hill.

Write about wasting.

Don't write about wasting.

Describe being overheated.

Write about the 10-day forecast.

Write about green tea.

Use 'Urge.'

Urge.

Write about childhood.

Write about the caw of crows.

Describe plenty.

Write about airplanes.

Write about 'The Economy of Trauma.'

Don't write about trauma.


Write about starting again.
         About starting new.
         About not starting.

Use grains of rice.

Write about your ear wax.

Write about claustrophobia.

Write it down.

Don't write it down.

Describe luxury.

# Number Nineteen: While making vegan brownies and listening to a podcast about Anna Nicole Smith.

Write about maligned women.

Write about what is healthy.

Write about what is unhealthy.

Write about the 90's.
       About being a kid in the 90's.
       About dial up internet.
       About what you remember of Anna Nicole Smith.

Use 'You're Wrong About.'

You're wrong about.

Describe reality.

Explain reality.

Write about The Jerry Springer Show.

Write about chocolate.

Use 'Flax.'

Flax.

Write about drugs.
       About drugs you've used.
       About drugs you miss.
       About why you don't do drugs anymore.

Write about aging.

Write about streaming television shows.

Use 'Precocious.'

Precocious.

Use 'Precaution.'
Precaution.

Caution.

Write about Fahrenheit vs Celsius.

Write about odours.

Use 'Aroma' instead.

Aroma.

Write about breast implants.

Write about your breasts.

# Number Twenty: After ordering a bunch of books. Some from Amazon. Some from a local bookstore.

Write about convenience.

Use 'Complicit.'

Complicit.

Write about the ice cream van's music.

Use 'Haunting.'

Haunting.

Write about not being a student.

Write about reading.

Read.

Write about Eileen Myles.

Write about embarrassment.

Write about anxiety.
        About panic attacks.
        About disassociation.

Write about how you hate amazon.

Write about why you still use it.

Don't write about why you still use is.

Describe fast culture.

Write about depression shopping.

Write about the $100 your grandmother sent you for your birthday.

Use 'Exchange Rate.'

Exchange.

Rate.

Write about blue sky.

Write about flowers.

Use the term 'Nosegay.'

Write about Females by Andrea Long Chu.

Describe walking.

Describe walking with Rebecca Solnit.

Describe walking the same path.

Write about sex games.

Write about not eating.

Don't write about not eating.

Use a pair of tweezers.

Use 'Deliberate.'

Deliberate.

## Number Twenty-one: After getting back in bed (fully dressed) in the afternoon because it was one of those days.

Describe gray.

Describe dark.

Write about cold to the bone.

Write about the smell of baking granola.

Explain fatigue.

Use 'Fatigue.'

Fatigue.

Use the phrase "One of those flexible fat girls.'

One of those.

Flexible.

Fat Girls.

Write about tights.

Write about *The Covent Garden Ladies* by Hallie Rubenhold.

Write about zoom calls.

Write about explicit content.

Use 'All You Can Do.'

All you can do.

Can do.

Write about more rain.

Explain slump.

Use a brown crayon.

Write about ticket stubs.
        About ticket stubs you collect.
        About ticket stubs as bookmarks.
        About missing tickets.

Don't write about how much telly you watch.

Write about how much telly you watch.

Make up new words.

Write about fascination.

# Number Twenty-two: While writing with friends via zoom after watching Biden's inauguration.

Write about new modes of communication.

Write about people you wouldn't have met without the pandemic.

Use 'Grateful.'

Grateful.

Write about the age of Aquarius.

Write about being an Aquarius.

Write about crying once a day.

Describe Magic.

Write about crushes on people.

Don't write about crushes on people.

Write about *Educated* by Tara Westover.

Write about Mormons.

Write about staining your pillow with tears.

Use 'Radical Shift.'

Radical.

Shift.

Write about the lesser of two evils.

Use lyrics to a song.

Don't use exclamation points.

Write about a bird broach.

## Number Twenty-Three: After talking to granny on the phone for two hours.

Write about soul mates.

Write about talking about nothing.

Use 'Our bond is not dependent on your knowing.'

Our bond is not dependent on your knowing.

Write about exchange of ideas.

Describe missing.

Write about love.
>About being loved.
>About loving.
>About unconditional love.

Use 'Happy Birthday.'

Happy Birthday.

Write about time differences.

Write about cake.

Use 'When I see you.'

When I see you.

Describe how she knew.

Write about having a full brain.

Write about small still lives.

Write about routine.

Explain reverence.

Write a first draft.

Don't write a first draft.

Use invisible ink.

Write about online shopping.
    About justifying purchases.
    About buyer's remorse.
    About the shame of shopping.

Write about *Lowborn* by Kerry Hudson.

Write about how long six months is.

Write about how long six months feels.

Don't write about six months.

# Number Twenty-Four: On the day of a birthday.

Write about age.

Write about looking young.

Write about feeling old.

Write about takeaways.

Use 'Back to normal.'

Don't use 'Back to normal.'

Write about depressing conversations.

Write about birthday ennui.

Write about gratitude.

Explain contemplation.

Write about what you are scared of.

Use 'Just like this.'

Just.

Like.

This.

Describe the feeling of being about to cry.

Write about a change of scenery.

Write about feeling the weight of it.

About whatever it is.
About whatever it was.
About it.

Write about casual drug use.

Write about ten years ago.

Don't write about ten years ago.

Use 'A morning spooning.'

Morning/Spooning.

Write about the emptiness after zoom meetings.

Write about Oscar Wilde.

Use the quote ' To begin to love one's self is the start of a lifelong romance.'

To begin.

To love one's self.

Start.

Lifelong romance.

## Number Twenty-Five: After reading Jenny Slate's *Little Weirds* on a bench in the park when it was sunny but freezing.

Write about mittens vs gloves.

Describe being unincumbered.

Use 'Weird.'

Weird.

Write about perseverance.

Write about the smell of applesauce.

Write about people watching.
      About people holding hands.
      About people without coats.
      About people with cups.
      About people running.

Write about menu planning.

Describe spontaneous.

Write about being wild.

Write about the code of Hammurabi.

Use 'To have and to hold.'

To have.

To hold.

Write about the unwritten pages.

Describe 100,000.

Write about blame.

Write about readjusting.

Use a small piece of paper.

Write about not getting dressed.

Write about a wild boar with orange feathers.

Write a letter to yourself.
        From your ego.
        From your heart.
        From your dreams.
        From your stomach.

Write over words you've already written.

Use 'Inferno.'

Inferno.

# Number Twenty-Six: Upon waking up with that feeling of dread that has no explanation.

Write about it.

Don't write about it.

Write about decaying lilies.

Write about your electric blanket breaking.

Write about not showering, again.

Use 'Fed Up'

Fed.

Up.

Write about getting on with it.

Write about tomorrow.

Write about whatever you can.

Use 'Stagnant.'

Stagnant.

# Number Twenty-Seven: After finishing watching *It's A Sin*.

Write about Keith Haring.
    About seeing his exhibition in Liverpool.
    About the bumper sticker on your mom's car.
    About the t-shirt you had when you were five.

Write about what you remember.

Describe what you forgot.

Write about being too young.
    About being too young for some things.
    About being old enough for others.

Write about Freddy Mercury.

Write about missing queer spaces.

Use 'Parallels.'

Parallels.

Describe grieving the world.

Write about misinformation.

Write about the meaning of foil.

Use a piece of cardboard.

Write about stopping.

Write about not stopping.

# Number Twenty-Eight: After dressing up for the first time in months.

Write about image.

Write about Fashion.

Write about the way your lips feel with lipstick.

Write about the day you binged watched *Project Runway*.

Use 'This body now!'

This body now!

Explain Dark Academia

Write about lesbians in the 1940's.

Write about feeling good.

Write about caring.

Write about not caring.

Explain the difference.

Use a Venn diagram.

Write about oversized.

Write about retail therapy.

Write about therapy.

Describe appearance.

Write about Etsy.                                    Write about tweed.

Number Twenty-Nine: After a week
of hard news from friends back home
that you haven't seen in over a year
and a half.

Write about how a day feels like a month.

Write about how a month feels like a week.

Write about melting ice.

Write about teleportation.

Use 'If Only.'

If Only.

Describe friendship.

Write about running into your ex-lover in the park.
    About how it is the first person you have seen in two weeks.
    About how you wish it hadn't been.

Write about *Peace Train* by Cat Stevens.

Explain repeated cycles.

Write about wishing.

Write about supporting people.

Use two tin cans and a piece of string.

Write about comfort for the comforter.

Use 'When I see you'

When I see you.

When I.

See you.

Write about not dreaming.

Write about separation.

Explain separation.

Write about home.

Use 'Emotionally complex.'

Emotionally.

Complex.

## Number Thirty: On a cold dreich day and not going on a walk.

Write about jumpers.

Write about sweaters.

Use slang terms.

Write about submitting.
  About submitting your writing.
  About submitting to.
  About submission.

Describe catching up.

Write about how this ends.

Write about playing words with friends.

Use questions.

Don't use answers.

Write about freezing rain.

Write about Valentine's Day.

Write about "You got this."

Don't write about "You got this."

Write about pastilles.

Use a green marker.

Write about booking train tickets.

Describe silence.

Write about typing.

Write about *Trans* by Jack Halberstam.

Use 'Endless love.'

Endless love.

First published in 2022 by orangeapplepress

orangeapplepress is run between Canada and Scotland.

Editors: Meredith Grace Thompson & T. Person.

www.orangeapplepress.com

Printed in Great Britain
by Amazon

83426065R00038